# Seeds

Rebekah Smith

BookLeaf Publishing

India | USA | UK

Presentation by *BookLeaf Publishing*

Web: www.bookleafpub.com

E-mail: info@bookleafpub.com

ISBN: 978-93-5744-833-8

First edition 2022

To those that have given me Love and taken
mine...


let's continue.

# Useful

Like a seed
you will feel small
buried
down
invisible and ignorant
on where you could grow

There is comfort in dirt
under mountains you have built
over yourself

I am shredding apart every piece
of Love in reach
to scatter and sow
all of my own
to be deeply rooted
to make use of being
low

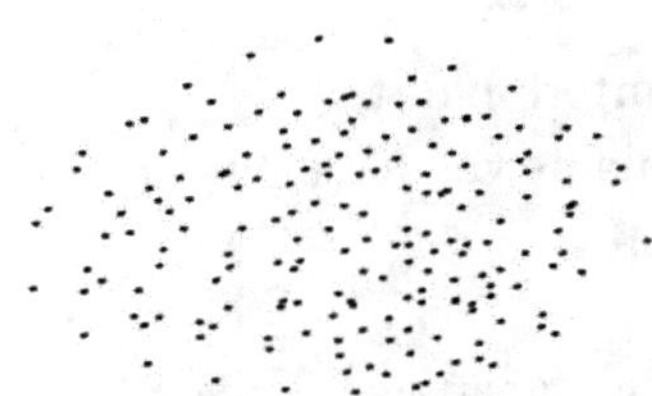

# Selfishly free

We see miracles and signs
through our lives
and still we're free
to believe in our own
selfish finds

What would it take...
a thrill or a mistake
to plant our minds as well
as our feet?

# Hiding

I'm worried I can't
keep myself
covered
Constantly hiding
to be free

Every better thing scares me of what else
it could bring
Brought on myself
wanting
getting
losing
always something else

Help
me
breathe
where I am
Help me see
what I can

# Holding on

I exhaust myself to not knowing where I am
This time is so small compared
to what is yet to come
what I've already done

If there would be
less of me and more of God
maybe
I could hear the right words
sing the right song
think the right thought

God knows where I belong
where I've been
what is gone

Help me remember
help me know I'm not alone

Lost is the last thought I think
before I sleep
lost is me
yet still what I need
So sure of nothing
so tired of disbelief
I run

after the smallest things
because of this constant need to be
more
Holding onto truth would be easy
if it would ever hold me back

# Circles

Tracing circles
with your index
in the dark of your home
to continue and complete
anything
A sentence..
a thought..
circulating your heart

I have never seen
such sadness before me
If taking
your darkness should leave
me heartless
I would make it
my own
before I felt another beat

# Cold, half empty

Sitting like company
in my own home
on the edge of my seat
sipping lightly
on a cold,
half empty
cup of coffee

Wondering
what to say
what to do

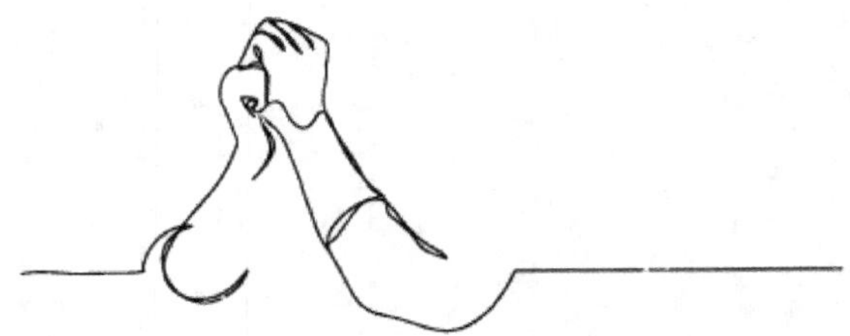

# Fake flowers

Fake flowers are incredibly upsetting...

Plant them in a barren setting
or hang them high
up on your wall
to trick your guests
to trick them all
Awes and admirers come and go
still
fake flowers will not grow
You won't find any weeds or roots
no pollution to dilute
Only blossoms
silence and decor

What did we bother
fake flowers for?

# It

If I let myself
rot from the inside out
no one would ever know
everyone would doubt
She was lovely, she was kind
gave others fair chance to speak their minds
No,
never would they know
on the surface of my bones
is a scum that won't leave me
alone

It holds on as if
it's scared
of itself, of me
I feel it
holding back breath
to not wake anything

Maybe
there is something close
and it knows
if it lets
air into my lungs that isn't
drenched in filth
it

would be forced
to rebuild
commanded to
still
my shaking
clear
my mind
heal
my body

I have known what
I have
but always thought
it
was bad

# LDL

You were proud of me
when I got that worthless
job
You laughed with me
when I had nothing
at all
You drew for me
when my mind wouldn't
allow my hands
to move
just right

I wish you were here
to write my lines
for me
right now

# Protected

I pray for what I don't have
and abandon what I do
A form of abuse
that I use to protect
what I want as truth

Uncertainty takes
my breath away
though I give it
sometimes
too

God, give me rest in you
Turn fear into hope
even in the unknown
I don't mean to be ungrateful
I just want to be home

# Light

There are thin places
where light can shine through
Could be
a glitch in design
but I think it's with you

When you know your mom is truly laughing
loudly
or when I hear that song
you always
said could ground me

My mind clears like a coastline
whenever we entwine

You barely kiss my life
and my soul is fortified

# On time

Breathing in grace
a morning reminds me
I'm not too late
You're allowed to be new
over and always
let air through

Set your heart
on fire
burn for all you have built

# Yes

Not necessarily never say never
not now or not no
Notice this
and know it will happen
someday
but not necessarily
how you have always
known

# Strong tomorrow

Remember here?
Wanting and waiting
to be where you are
now
It's time
to believe and trust
you are not a waste
Everything will
be okay
yesterday, tomorrow, today

Little by little
you'll solve the riddle
Expect your bones
dry as dust
to rise up
strong as stone

Wrong
will wash away
Strength will stay

# Listening

I have worried far too much
about opinions that aren't mine
that I don't yet know what I'm like

Suffocating in soons
bruised in my own misuse
because I don't say much
to myself anymore

I Love the sounds
of things without words
I have gone
far too long without
just feeling
sometimes forgetting
about my Love

I do
need it back

# Playful

Remembering you
brings
a feeling like youth

on a swing in the yard
restlessly flying
breathless and blue
repetitively wanting

higher
Again

# To you and I

You deserved to be
safe
instead you became
strong

You are better than before
even though you feel wrong

It will take time
to know safety again
but your strength is yours
when you begin to trust your defense

Lend an ear
be a friend
don't let the light leave your eyes
again
Rest
as you need
but know you don't have to
Yourself is yours
your body has made amends

Love is around you
its roots are buried deeply
Don't loosen your mind on what is true

what is you

Be safe,
my Love,
stay yours
Let your mind know it is not alone in knowing
where you have been

You will live
for reason
for Love
for you

Your body is beautiful
your mind is used

# Getting to know

Peace
with me
and also with you

something new

beautiful
beyond current belief

Water by a home
a Love that mends alone
more
than we have ever known

sturdy and safe
something right
for a change

something good
to settle our bones

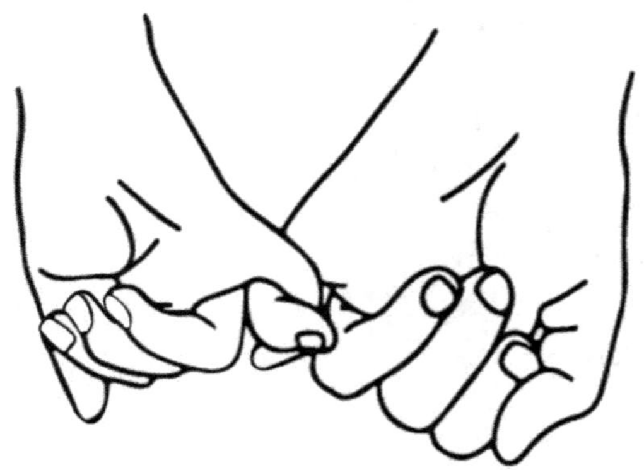

# Forgiven

Jump to new conclusions
ones that let you feel well

the time to flee is over
be what others need
and you will be free

Don't dwell on your faults
don't forget you're forgiven

It really is okay
if you go
or stay

# Better

If there was a map of how you would grow
would you still go?
I would have stopped to rest
a long time alone
if I had known how
this would change me
and what I would have to believe in
not knowing how
I would need this
to see it
is all going to work
for good

it has to
it should

When in heaven
would I regret?
Why not try
to let it make you break
your heart up to see
what it's made up of
Push your buttons
see how you work

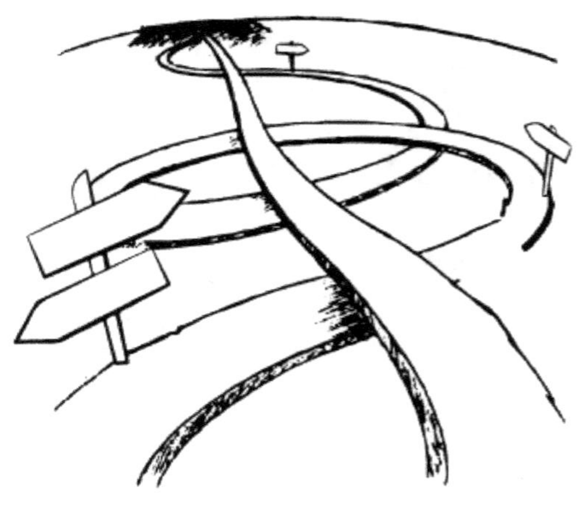

# Know me by my fruit

I will get my worth in vines
with all the time I did not waste

I am lucky there is Love for me
or I wouldn't
I couldn't be
I wouldn't breathe

I am pruned to believe
my leaves are now fruit

I have no hunger
except to know me
to be useful
not used
picking myself
to give first

Not fallen
not bruised
ripe and full of life